, A   ise, *Last Things*)

Samuel French—London
New York-Toronto-Hollywood

Acting Exercise ©

Humour Helps, Waiting for a Bu

Rights of Performance by Ama

52 Fitzroy Street, London W1

issue licences to amateurs on p

Copyright to give any perf

before the fee has been paid

The Royalty Fee indicated b

variation at the sole discretion of

Basic fee for each and every p

in the British Isles

Humour Helps Code C

Waiting for a Bus Code D

Acting Exercise Code B

Last Things Code C

Corpsing (all four plays) Code M

The Professional Rights in these plays are controlle

RAMSAY LTD, 60 Wardour Street, London W1V 4ND.

ISBN 0 573 10006 3

Please see page vi for further copyright information

CORPSING

A volume of three duologues and one three-hander which encapsulates Peter Barnes' consummate skill of contrasting opposites and simultanously combining "the absurdly tragic and the tragically absurd".

In *Humour Helps* an actress hamfistedly tries to commit suicide, finally achieving her aim with the unwitting aid of a neighbour.

Waiting for a Bus has a pair of lovers interrupted in bed by the arrival of the husband — or are they actors rehearsing a new comedy *Waiting for a Bus* about a pair of lovers disturbed by the husband's arrival ...?

Acting Exercise opens with Rowan, an actor, delivering a soliloquy in a rehearsal room. From the shadows emerges a distraught husband demanding the actor give him back his wife. With a superlative performance, Rowan convinces the husband he is mistaken, but alone again he crows: "I could sell electric fans to Eskimos!"

In *Last Things* an elderly couple of thespians awake in bed to find themselves dead. Troupers that they are, they decide to go into the next world with their famous husband and wife sketch — to the applause of the heavenly host.

CONTENTS

HUMOUR HELPS

CHARACTERS

Hilda Grayson
Saunders

The action takes place in a modern apartment

HUMOUR HELPS

An immaculate, beautifully furnished, fifth-floor apartment, complete with subdued lighting, a white floor, gleaming table and white mugs R, *and french windows* L

Hilda Grayson sits on a sofa C, *drunk. She has been crying and drinking. There is a large half-empty bottle of whisky, a knife and a perfectly arranged plate of food on the table in front of her. A double-barrelled shotgun is wrapped in a long cardboard parcel under the table. The waste-paper basket on the floor beside her is filled with used Kleenex tissues*

Taking another drink, she reads a much crumpled letter, suddenly lets out a great despairing cry, and tears up the letter in a fury

Hilda No more! ... I can't bear it! ... Where has tenderness gone?! ...

She opens her handbag, empties the contents on the sofa and picks up a bottle of pills

I'm prepared, thick and thin ... End of the line, hitting the buffers ... I'm a brain blow-out, an inside-out schizophrenic, a head-to-tail spade-headed looney. My mind scratches glass ...

Grasping the arm of the sofa she heaves herself up and tries to open the bottle of pills

But the screw-top sticks and she turns it frantically, "click-click-click". As she struggles violently with it she knocks over the waste basket

She suddenly completely loses her temper and throws the bottle on the glass table, smashing the bottle to pieces, and spilling pills all over the floor. Cursing to herself, she falls on her knees to scramble for them, but instead crushes dozens of them into the carpet

Another dead day ... I want to spit in somebody's eye ... I've got a difficulty for every solution ... Go away, I don't want you!

She suddenly jumps up and grabs the knife from the table

She holds out her arm which waves violently and shakily brings the sharp knife to her left wrist. Closing her eyes, she slashes herself violently

As blood drips over the white floor, Hilda opens her eyes, sways, and groans loudly at the sight of the blood — and then discovers she has only cut her thumb

Why me? ... Why pick on me? ... The dark drives me on! ... Let me do it!

She stares at her bleeding thumb for a moment, then sticks it in her mouth and staggers back to the sofa still clutching the knife

She takes her thumb out of her mouth, takes a swig of whisky, and without warning plunges the knife into her chest

Unfortunately it doesn't even penetrate her expensive thick sweater

You see! ... That's what I've had to put up with!

In a fury she throws the knife down on the plate which smashes to pieces

She then sees that her bleeding thumb has spattered blood all over the carpet

Filthy! ... Filthy!

She wraps a pile of Kleenex round her thumb and tries to rub out the blood on the carpet with some of the used Kleenex

She suddenly stops

What do I care?! ... I'm going to die!

She pulls a long cardboard parcel from under the table

Once I put my mind to something ... I follow through ... Nothing stops me ... Nothing!

She rips open the parcel and takes out a double-barrelled shotgun and two cartridges without noticing she has knocked over a vase in her haste

I told them I was prepared ... No-one believed me ... Now they'll believe me ... Happiness and the pursuit thereof!

After taking another drink straight from the bottle, she clumsily breaks open the gun and inserts two cartridges. She closes the gun with great difficulty as the blood from her cut makes the gun handle slippery

This is the best way ... Do it *clean*! ... *Clean*!

Placing the muzzle of the gun under her chin, she bends down to fire it only to discover the gun is too long and she is too short to reach the trigger

What idiot made this thing?! ... Clean! ... Do it clean! ... *Clean*!

As she strains down to reach it, the gun falls over

It's a conspiracy! *Things*'re against me. It's always *things* ... People as well, but mostly things!

In utter frustration she tries to find a position where she can pull the trigger so she crouches down and wraps herself around the gun barrel, panting

Clean ... Do it clean! ... Absolutely clean!

She unwraps herself and tries kneeling with the gun, only to nearly poke her eye out with the weapon

Why have I always been like this? It takes me an hour to cook Minute rice so this is nothing new. I must be the living proof of reincarnation, no-one can be as dumb as me in one lifetime ... But I'll do it clean ... I will! I *will*! ...

She falls on her back, kicks off her shoes and tries to pull the trigger with her toes

But she can't so she lurches up, puts the gun at a grotesque angle and reaches down. Her hands get nearer and nearer the trigger. But her bloody fingers slip off, she knocks herself under her chin with the end of the gun barrel. Staggering back she finds the gun barrel entangled in her sweater

When things go wrong, there's nothing you can do about it, par for the course ...

In savagely pulling the barrel free, she puts the gun butt through the french window

After Hilda opens the window to extricate the gun she has another desperate idea

If I can just hook the trigger ... You've got to get up pretty early in the morning to beat me — about twelve noon!

She undoes her belt, puts the mouth of the gun under her chin and uses the buckle of the belt as a fish-hook to pull the trigger

Concentrate and you'll catch the big one ...

After a couple of attempts she manages to get the belt buckle round the trigger. She lets out a cry of triumph and then realizes her skirt is falling down

Don't you dare! ... Up, keep it up! ...

As she struggles to pull up her skirt, she inadvertently pulls the trigger, the gun fires, blasting a hole in the ceiling

As Hilda is showered with lumps of plaster, there is a cry of panic from the flat above and a leg comes crashing through the hole in the ceiling as someone above starts to fall through it

Covered with plaster and blood, her skirt falling down, Hilda looks round the once immaculate but now devastated room

She slumps to the floor in despair as the leg in the hole in the ceiling is painfully withdrawn, sending down another shower of plaster on her

A man's voice, Saunders', shouts down from above

Saunders (*off*) What're you doing down there?!
Hilda Trying to kill myself.
Saunders (*off*) What?
Hilda I'm trying to kill myself!
Saunders (*off*) Do you need any help?
Hilda No. I can do it myself.
Saunders (*off*) Would you like me to ring the Samaritans?
Hilda *Please*, anything but that! ...

Saunders' face appears, peering down through the hole in the ceiling

Saunders The name's Saunders ... You realize you've made a hole in my floor? I've just had it done — parquet.

Hilda I'm sorry.

Saunders I guess it was an accident. Nobody deliberately shoots a hole in somebody's floor.

Hilda No.

Saunders Would you like to come up for a drink? I've got to go out in half an hour, but we can have a quick one.

Hilda I've had a number of quick ones.

Saunders Do you still feel like doing ... ?

Hilda Oh, yes. I'm just getting my second wind.

Saunders You know it's going to be a lovely day tomorrow.

Hilda No, it's going to rain.

Saunders Is it? You can never take weather forecasts seriously. Shouldn't you take some medication or other. Valium maybe, or a placebo. You know I used to think a placebo was a Spanish singer. Listen, you should talk about this before you do anything too drastic. We're intelligent people. I'm sure we've got an IQ of 188 — between us, of course. I'll bet you can do Chinese take-aways in your head. What's your job?

Hilda I'm an actress.

Saunders Well, we all have our problems. My best friend's an actor. He hasn't had a part for two years but he can't give it up, after all it's his living ... My sister used to sing but she couldn't carry a tune if it had handles.

Hilda What about you?

Saunders I'm an unemployed history teacher — no class.

Hilda Tell me about the Battle of Hastings?

Saunders The what?

Hilda The Battle of Hastings.

Saunders 1066 ... Between Harold, King of England and William the Conqueror. Everybody knows the story ... Harold sitting on his horse with an arrow stuck in his eye and all his friends giving him advice like "Keep blinking, it'll soon work its way out" ... "Have you tried sneezing?" ...

Hilda laughs

There, that's better, isn't it?

Hilda No it isn't. Just because I'm laughing doesn't make it better. You made me laugh but the pain's still there. Laughter can't reach that deep.

Saunders I don't know what else to do. Laughter's supposed to be therapeutic. Do you want to tell me what's the matter?

Hilda No.

Saunders Thank God, I'd only get depressed! Anyway, never take the advice of a man in trouble ... I'll tell you about myself, if you want.

Hilda Why?

Saunders I'm trying to keep your interest and you might want to know how other people suffer too.

Hilda I don't want to know that.

Saunders But it'll help. You think you're the only one. Look at me, I've had it rough. It started when I was a baby. I looked an odd shape. My mother put shutters on my pram when she took me out. I've always been unlucky, if there is reincarnation I'll come back as myself after I'm dead. My family lived in Clerkenwell. What more can I say? They were dull. I think my father died when he was twenty but he was buried at seventy. Everything was grey, we used to drink grey orange juice. It's like England, grey all over. If it wasn't for mouth-to-mouth resuscitation, there'd be no romance in this country at all. But then I had a great idea, I got married. If you're for a long life and a slow death I can recommend marriage. I guess it's a good way for women to keep active, till the right man comes along. I asked if she'd love me when I was old and bald? And she said, "Don't ask, it's tough enough when you're young and hairy." On our honeymoon, she thought she could make me happy. After all, she'd made six men happy the week before. Of course, she left me. I spend my days alone up here. I get so lonely my echo doesn't even come back. My answering machine's died of rust. I wish I was a schizophrenic, I'd have somebody to talk to. Looking back over my life it's a one hundred per cent record of failure and ...

But Hilda has had enough. She suddenly jumps up, lets out a cry
of despair and rushes out through the open french window on to
the balcony and jumps

There is a faint cry and the sickening thud as her body hits the
ground below. There is a dying gasp and silence

Saunders continues talking to the empty room, his voice and the
Lights fading

Saunders Hello? ... Where are you? I can't see you ... You all right?
Was I boring you? ... Say something even if it's only goodbye ...
Should I keep talking? ... I think I should ... Talk I mean ... But I'll
keep it light and funny ... Humour helps, it's what keeps us going,
isn't it? ...

Black-out

FURNITURE AND PROPERTY LIST

On stage: Sofa. *On it*: handbag containing various items including
              bottle of pills
              Table. *On it*: white mugs, vase, half-empty bottle of whisky,
              box of Kleenex, plate (breakable) of food, knife. *Beside it*:
              waste-paper basket full of used Kleenex. *Under it*: double-
              barrelled shotgun and 2 cartridges in cardboard parcel
              Crumpled letter for **Hilda**

Personal: **Hilda**: blood sac

LIGHTING PLOT

Property fittings required: nil

To open: Full general lighting

Cue 1   **Saunders**: "Hello? ..."   (Page 10)
            Begin fade to black-out

EFFECTS PLOT

Cue 1   **Hilda** struggles to pull up her skirt   (Page 7)
         Blast from shotgun

Cue 2   Faint cry from **Hilda** as she falls   (Page 10)
         Thud of body hitting ground

WAITING FOR A BUS

CHARACTERS

Tony Chapman
Jane Bryner
Paul Bryner

The action takes place in what looks like a bedroom

WAITING FOR A BUS

A double bed C and a wardrobe one side, and a dressing-table on the other

Tony Chapman and Jane Bryner are lying half undressed on the bed

Chapman Let me answer your question.

Jane I haven't asked you one.

Chapman I know but I'd still like to answer it. I love you, darling, and coming from me that's a compliment. But if your husband finds out about our affair, I'll have to face the combined might of "Shakey, Sharkey and Quinch". We're both lawyers so I know just how unpleasant he could make it.

Jane Who started it? You took me to dinner and came on with the line, "I think you'll find this an excellent Bordeaux and me witty and urbane with it." Remember I laughed? I hadn't laughed since the previous Easter. My husband may be a legal giant but outside the courts he's a black hole of fun.

Chapman I heard him speak once. He was as boring as the House of Lords laid end to end.

Jane It got to the stage I was just sitting and watching my fingernails grow.

Chapman Poor darling, you don't deserve that. There's no justice in the world, though speaking as a lawyer I'm sure that's not entirely a bad thing.

Jane There are so many mysteries in life, so many hidden links, unseen powers that draw two people like us together. No laws can withstand the fury of what I feel for you.

They embrace passionately

Chapman There's no happiness in the world compared to our love.
Jane You are my life, my soul, I breathe you.
Chapman Nothing can separate us, no cord can hold us as fast as
   love does.

There is a sound off

Jane Did you hear that?
Chapman What?
Bryner (*off*) Hello!
Jane My husband!

*Chapman shoots off the bed, grabbing his trousers, shoes and
jacket*

Bryner (*off*) Darling, are you still here?

*Panicking, Chapman tries to hide under the bed but Jane pulls him
out*

Jane Yes!

She points to the wardrobe. Chapman dives inside just as:

   Paul Bryner comes into the bedroom

Bryner Would you believe it I forgot ... what's wrong?
Jane Wrong? There's nothing wrong.
Bryner I thought you were going out.
Jane I had a slight headache.

*Bryner picks up Chapman's tie left on the bed. Before she can stop
him, he opens the wardrobe and puts the tie on the rack, completely
ignoring the frightened figure of Chapman standing there, clutching
his clothes. Bryner closes the wardrobe*

Bryner Odd ... I thought I saw a ...

He opens the wardrobe again and stares at Chapman

   I did! What're you doing there?!
Chapman Waiting for a bus.

Bryner nods, shuts the wardrobe for a second, then wrenches it open again

Bryner Waiting for a bus?! In my wardrobe? Do you know who I
   am?
Chapman Yes. Do you know who I am?
Bryner No.
Chapman Thank God.
Bryner Waiting for a bus?! What's happening, Jane?
Jane It's obvious. I'm in bed and there's a man standing half-
   dressed in the wardrobe waiting for a bus.
Bryner Waiting for a ... waiting for a ... *ahhhh.*

Clutching his chest Bryner suddenly slumps to the floor. Chapman comes out of the wardrobe as Jane scrambles off the bed. They bend down beside Bryner

Chapman Is something wrong?
Jane What is it?

Bryner suddenly sits up

Bryner Waiting for a bus ...
Jane What?
Bryner Waiting for a bus. That's what's wrong. Let me try it.

He gets up. He goes into the wardrobe and closes the door. Chapman shrugs and Jane goes back on the bed. Chapman repeats Bryner's line

Chapman Odd ... I thought I saw a ...

He opens the wardrobe, and stares at Bryner

   I did! What're you doing there?!
Bryner Waiting for a bus.

Chapman nods, shuts the wardrobe for a second, then wrenches it open again

Chapman Waiting for a bus?! In my wardrobe? Do you know who I am?
Bryner Yes. Do you know who I am?
Chapman No.
Bryner Thank God.
Chapman Waiting for a bus? What's happening, Jane?
Jane It's obvious. I'm in bed and there's a man standing half-dressed in the wardrobe, waiting for a bus.
Chapman Waiting for a ... waiting for a ... *ahhh*.

Clutching his chest, he slumps to the floor. Bryner comes out of the wardrobe and Jane scrambles off the bed

Bryner Is something wrong?
Jane What is it?
Bryner Waiting for a bus. That's still what's wrong ... Waiting for a bus ... Och ay, I'm waiting for a bus, de yer ken ... Sure it's meself who's waiting for a bus, yer honour ... So vat does it look like I'm doing? I'm vaiting for a bus, oi vey ... I thought maybe an accent might help. It doesn't. It's still wrong. You're hiding in a wardrobe. I ask you what you're doing there and you say "I'm waiting for a bus."
Chapman Yes.
Bryner I don't believe it.
Jane You can believe it'll get a laugh.
Bryner I don't want a laugh.
Chapman What did you say?!
Jane You can't be serious?!

Chapman Are you actually telling us you don't want a laugh?

Bryner Er, well, not necessarily.

Chapman You must be mad, Paul. We want all the laughs we can get.

Bryner Not cheap ones, Tony.

Chapman Laughs never come cheap, you have to sweat blood to get 'em.

Jane Cheap or expensive, laughs are laughs. And you can keep your booze, crack, smack, coke and sex, there's nothing in the world as satisfying as a big fat boffo.

Bryner There are laughs and laughs. When Stalin laughed, people had heart attacks.

Chapman What is it, Paul? People say you and Jane are the best husband and wife comedy team in the business. And with all due modesty, I have a reputation as *the* comic actor of his generation. We know how to make 'em laugh — and if they don't, screw 'em.

Jane It's because you're directing the play, isn't it, Paul? That's why you've gone intellectual.

Bryner I don't want a low-brow show for high-grade morons. I'd like us to be "true" and "real" as well as funny.

Chapman True ... Real ... No bums on seats with true and real.

Bryner All I want is for us to be truly sincere in our playing.

Jane I've spent all my acting life trying to be sincerely insincere.

Chapman Dangerous ground, Paul. When I was in weekly rep we were doing *Rookery Nook*. We had a famous farce actor as guest. On the first night he delivered his opening line and got his laugh but before I could reply he tugged at my sleeve and whispered ... "Not yet, laddie ... don't say your line yet ... not yet ... not yet ... say it now!" I said it and got the biggest laugh ever, before or since.

Bryner I'm not saying technique and timing aren't important — they are. But fuelled with true feeling. Real comedy has its roots in life and I say the line "waiting for a bus" is rootless.

Jane You're the director, ask the author to change it.

Bryner Can't. After all, he's called the play *Waiting for a Bus* so he must think the line important. Besides, we don't want the author hanging about here anymore than we have to.

Jane God no!

Chapman We agree there.

Bryner The line is just a symptom of the larger problem with the whole scene. For once, it isn't a writing but an acting problem. That's why I got us here for a Saturday rehearsal. Just the three of us alone, on stage, away from the stage management and the rest of the company.

Jane I don't know if it's going to help unless we know what you want.

Bryner I want you to recognize the pain inherent in that line, this scene.

Chapman Set it to music, and we'll sing it. Paul, this is a comedy called *Waiting for a Bus*, not *Godot* or *Oedipus Rex*.

Bryner If it was it'd be easier. Lies are an important part of tragedy, the lies that con us into believing stinking corpses are noble remains. Comedy is truth telling. Besides it's a new play. That makes it really hard. Nobody has ever played these characters before so there's nobody to tell us how. Whereas thousands of actors have played Hamlet.

Chapman No wonder people think he's crazy.

Jane You still haven't told us what you want.

Bryner I'm not going to tell you anything. I want us to discover it for ourselves. I'm not going to behave like every other director, treating actors like so much silly putty.

Jane Over-educated traffic wardens. Remember that last one we worked with who kept miming batting strokes all through rehearsals? (*She mimes*) Leg break ... cut ... off drive ...

Chapman I had one who kept tearing off hundreds of bits of masking tape and rolling them into little balls like a nervous dung-beetle.

Jane But power lies in their hands now and if a slug wears a crown you must always bow low.

Chapman The nerve and gall of these people.

Bryner That's one of the reasons I'm directing this play. I know your needs. After all, I am an actor myself ... What? You said something ...?

Jane Nothing.

Bryner I want you to work to the very limits of your personalities
and intelligence. Here we have a routine situation, but a situation
however routine has unique properties which apply to that
situation alone. Now, an adulterer is discovered hiding in the
wardrobe by the deceived husband who asks him what he is doing
there? The adulterer reacts in total confusion. Confusion is the
emotion to play, you understand?

Jane Confusion. Totally.

Bryner Not you — him. You are given the proposition —
confusion. Confusion occurs in your soul and passes deep into
your whole being. It envelops you, eliminating all other precon-
ceptions ... Jesus, look at the time, I've got to meet Arne. Let's
break for lunch. Darling, I'll see you in Luigi's in half an hour.
Join us, Tony? No ... no ... right. Be back here at two-thirty. Don't
despair, we're making real progress. The yeast is rising, the pie is
baking.

He exits quickly

Chapman stamps around the stage grimacing

Chapman Pretentious! Pretentious! Pretentious!

Jane With Paul you can always hear the sound of hammers missing
nuts.

Chapman Your husband has the personality of a temporary filling.
How do you put up with him?

They start getting undressed again

Jane It isn't easy. Did you see how he ignored me? I'm in the scene
too. My reaction to you in the wardrobe is vital. He's no director,
even though he can't stop talking.

Chapman He's certainly no actor. He couldn't call his dog and
make it believable. How dare he patronize me. I'm a bigger name
than him. People know me.

Jane They know me, too.
Chapman I'm only doing this because of you.

They kiss passionately

Jane And is he grateful? Doesn't know the meaning of the word.
  He's using us.
Chapman All his talk of "real" and "true" means the play is going
  to be about as light as a lead balloon by the time he's finished with
  it.
Jane He can be awesomely untalented at times. He's way above his
  head. Don't forget we've only got half an hour.

They lie on the bed

Chapman I need your husband like I need three elbows.
Jane He retired temporarily last year because of illness and fatigue
  — the public were sick and tired of him.
Chapman He's destroying this play. And that's a pity. It's quite
  good.
Jane Some of the lines sing. What's that one of yours — "There's
  no happiness in the world compared to our love."
Chapman "You are my life, my soul, I breathe you."
Jane "Nothing can separate us, no cord can hold us as fast as love
  does."

They embrace and roll over. Chapman suddenly looks up

Chapman Did you hear that?
Jane That's my line. What do you say now?
Chapman What?
Jane What?
Bryner (*off*) Hello!
Jane My husband!

*Chapman frantically scrambles off the bed grabbing some of his
clothes*

Bryner (*off*) Darling, are you still here?

Panicking, Chapman tries to hide under the bed. Jane pulls him away

Jane Yes!

As Bryner is heard approaching, Chapman instinctively dives into the wardrobe just as:

Bryner enters

Bryner Would you believe it, I forgot ... what's wrong?
Jane Wrong? There's nothing wrong.
Bryner I thought you were going out.
Jane I had a slight headache.

Seeing Chapman's tie left on the bed, Bryner picks it up and before Jane can stop him opens the wardrobe door, puts the tie on the rack, seemingly ignoring Chapman standing there half-dressed. He closes the wardrobe door, then frowns and opens it again

Bryner What're you doing there?
Chapman Waiting for a bus.
Bryner Oh ... Waiting for a bus? In my wardrobe? Do you know who I am?
Chapman Yes ... I mean no ... I mean, do you know who I am?
Bryner No.
Chapman You don't? ... thank God ... I'm confused ... what are we playing?
Bryner No, that won't do.
Jane What won't do?
Bryner Waiting for a bus. That's not the right way either. I still don't believe it. It's worse.
Chapman Worse?

He comes out of the wardrobe

Bryner The feeling's still wrong.

Chapman You'll never ever see me playing this scene with so much feeling.

Jane Nor me. For a moment there I was genuinely frightened.

Chapman And confused. It was real. As real as you'll ever get.

Bryner Hhmm.

Chapman Hhmm? If you can't see that was real — I'm walking out of this production. I mean it, Paul!

Jane Me too.

They start dressing

Bryner Well, it did have a certain rough spontaneity. But it was blurry, uncertain, as if you weren't acting with any clear intentions.

Jane That was your fault. You didn't stick to the script. You made cuts in the dialogue. Where was "Odd ... I thought I saw ... I did ..."?

Chapman And you cut comic business. You didn't shut the wardrobe after "Waiting for a bus", and then open it. You put both Jane and me totally off-balance.

Bryner I was improvising. I didn't come back to play the scene.

Jane Why did you come?

Bryner I forgot my briefcase. But when I saw you were rehearsing again it was too good to miss. I decided to speed it up, cut all extraneous business and get to the nitty-gritty — you hiding in the wardrobe.

Jane I thought we coped very well considering we weren't expecting you back.

Chapman We certainly weren't.

Bryner That's what gave the scene that rough spontaneity. But it's not important.

Chapman What is?

Bryner That I discovered you two as lovers.

Chapman What?

Bryner Right?

Jane Yes, right.

Bryner That's what's important about the scene. And I've got to say it, though your approach was different, most of your reactions were still strictly from stock ... the open mouth look, the eyes wide in horror, the frightened scuffling, the long pauses and grunts before beginning the line "Waiting for a bus". The pie-crust didn't rise. There was nothing truly real there, dear friends. All second-hand roses.

Jane Not real? Second-hand? How can you be so wrong?

Chapman You'll never hear "Waiting for a bus" delivered with such conviction or the whole scene played with such genuine emotion. Maybe you should take a look at your performance, Paul. Now that was second-hand roses.

Jane As the wronged husband you just weren't there. I could smell the greasepaint.

Bryner And I can smell the sour smell of sour grapes.

Chapman I'm convinced Jane and I would've convinced anyone we were lovers. We caught the precise mixture of fear and absurdity, panic and pathos needed to make that scene truly real.

Bryner Sorry, but it wasn't real for me — or funny.

Jane Not funny? That's a terrible thing to say to anyone, Paul.

Chapman I'll tell you how funny and real it was — Jane and I *are* lovers!

Bryner I know that.

Chapman Not in the play!

Bryner No, certainly not in the play. Not yet.

Jane In life you idiot!

Chapman You caught us really making love!

Bryner And I didn't believe it — right.

Jane But it's true. We were at it when you came back!

Bryner If that's "at it", it was pretty lack-lustre.

Chapman Lack-lustre, lack-lustre!

Jane I've loved Tony for years.

Bryner Try another one.

Chapman I only took this part to be near Jane.

Bryner I thought it was the chance to work with me.

Chapman *Ahhh* — the ego of the man!

Jane And I only agreed to this play when I knew Tony was
   interested.

Bryner Are you sure it wasn't because I was directing?

Jane No, no, no!

Bryner Perhaps I have been blind ... it happens ... I don't need a
   house to fall on me. But I still can't believe it. You in bed, and a
   half-naked man in the wardrobe. That's the play, not life. But now
   you say it is. You've made it real at last. Eyes can lie but not the
   heart, the heart knows. I have to believe it, Jane. Jane ... what's
   happened? You were playing it wrong and now you're playing it
   right, but it's still wrong — and in a different way. Right and
   wrong, who can tell ... no wonder laughter dies in the air ... Once
   I could smile at "waiting for a bus". Now it isn't funny ... waiting
   for a ... *ahh* ...

He suddenly staggers and crashes to the floor. Jane screams

Jane Paul!

Chapman My God!

Jane It's not true, none of it's true.

Chapman Of course it isn't true. Just a joke.

Bryner sits up

Bryner But not funny. Admit it. I wasn't funny just as you weren't
   funny.

Jane Is this your idea of a joke?

Chapman It's not funny.

Bryner Just what I said. You and Tony pretended to be lovers. I
   pretended to believe you. Not very funny or convincing.

Jane Convincing enough.

Bryner No, none of it felt right. Not me, not you. The situation is
   too far-fetched to be realistic. It has to be played comedically.

Chapman That's exactly what I said at the start.

Bryner The difference is, now we know for certain the other way
   doesn't work. That's what rehearsals are for — experimenting,
   making mistakes. We've learnt a lot. And what we've learnt will

add depth to the scene. Even if we do play it for comedy. Let's do it one more time whilst we're still hot. Arne can wait. This is more important. The pie's cooking. The pastry's rising.

Jane and Chapman take their clothes off again

Chapman We'll go for the laughs this time.
Jane I'm sure it'll feel more comfortable that way — for all of us.
Chapman I've got a few bits of comic business I'd like to try.
Bryner This is the time for it. Pick it up from my entrance.

He exits

Chapman and Jane get into bed

Jane You are my life, my soul. I breathe you.
Chapman Nothing can separate us, no cord can hold us as fast as love does.

There is a sound, off

Jane Did you hear that?
Chapman What?
Bryner (*off*) Hello!
Jane My husband!

Chapman and Jane simultaneously leap into the air in fright. As Jane tries to hide under the blanket, Chapman's arm smashes right through the flimsy wooden headrest at the top of the bed. The whole rest comes away and becomes entangled in his arm as he tumbles off the bed. It stops him from hiding under the bed as Jane struggle with the blanket

Bryner (*off*) Darling, are you still here?

Jane finally gets rid of the blanket, picks up Chapman's clothes and flings them at him

Jane Yes!

Jane jumps up and down on the bed and points frantically to the wardrobe as Bryner is heard approaching. Chapman tries to dive inside but is hampered by the wooden headrest still hanging on his arm. He tears it off, throwing pieces of wood on to the floor before scrambling into the wardrobe. In his haste part of his jacket is left hanging out of the door

Bryner enters

Bryner Would you believe it, I forgot ... what's wrong?

He trips over the discarded blanket and staggers across the room. As he does so, Chapman quickly opens the wardrobe door and pulls in the jacket only to leave part of his shirt hanging out instead. Jane sees Chapman has also left a shoe on the bed. She grabs it and stuffs it down the front of her slip as Bryner gets up

Jane Wrong? There's nothing wrong.
Bryner I thought you were going out.
Jane I had a slight headache.

She suddenly leaps off the bed to get between Bryner and the shirt she sees protruding from the wardrobe, and the shoe falls out of her slip and crashes to the floor. She picks it up. Thinking it is his, Bryner takes it from her and crosses to the wardrobe to put it away. He sees the broken wooden slats of the headrest on the floor and picks some up

Bryner Termites! The place is riddled with ravenous termites. Did you know there are two tons of termites to every man, woman and child on earth?

He opens the wardrobe and puts the shoe away, nodding agreeably to the trembling figure of Chapman standing there clutching his trousers

Bryner Hello ... (*He shuts the wardrobe and turns away*) Odd ... I
    thought I saw a ... I did, I saw a ... (*He flings open the wardrobe
    door again*) What're you going there?!
Chapman Waiting for a bus!

*Raucous music as he lets go of his trousers which fall, leaving him
trembling in his underpants*

Bryner That's it! That's it!

The three spontaneously congratulate each other

Black-out

FURNITURE AND PROPERTY LIST

On stage: Double bed with flimsy wooden headrest. *On it*: pillows,
                sheets, blanket, **Jane**'s clothes, **Chapman**'s trousers, tie,
                jacket. *Beside it*: **Chapman**'s shoes
                Wardrobe

LIGHTING PLOT

Property fittings required: nil

Interior. The same scene throughout

To open: Full general lighting

Cue 1   The three spontaneously congratulate each other   (Page 31)
            Black-out

EFFECTS PLOT

Cue 1   **Chapman**: "Waiting for a bus!"   (Page 31)
            Raucous music

ACTING EXERCISE

CHARACTERS

Rowan
Geoffrey Willet

The action takes place in a rehearsal room

ACTING EXERCISE

A rehearsal room

Rowan Lying lips are an abomination to the Lord. Christ said, "I am the Truth!" Yet our lives are raised on lies and a wise man questions every statement except the legitimacy of his own birth. Save us Lord, I feel an Apocalypse coming on. For a liar usurps God's prerogative and recreates the world in his own image. The moral order's wrecked, objects lose their natural names, force becomes right, right wrong and every treachery an act of friendship ...

He stops as someone clears his throat over to the left. He notices, for the first time, a man, Geoffrey Willet, watching him from the shadows

Did you hear that? An actor of my experience should be able to speak heightened prose like that without betraying the character. It was an unfocused mass of emotion. And did you hear those tiny gaps I inserted into the dialogue to make it more important? And how I shouted instead of speeding it up? An audience would get the impression that life was like the theatre instead of the theatre like life. I've no conviction, no confidence. I am not believable. Wait a minute. I don't know you. You're not with the Company. What're you doing here?

Willet Give me back my wife.

Rowan What? I told them out there I didn't want to be disturbed. How did you get in?

Willet The doorman's corrupt. Give me back my wife.

Rowan Whenever I'm around the loonies come out of the woodwork. Who the devil're you?

Willet Geoffrey Willet. You know why I'm here.

Rowan No.

Willet You don't?

Rowan No.

Willet Well, there you are then! Give me back my wife.

Rowan Mr Willet, I don't know your wife. I'm rehearsing a new play. I've grabbed an hour to work by myself. Please go quietly.

Willet I can't move, my legs're dead. I've got the inside shakes. Give me back my wife.

Rowan Who is your wife?

Willet Muriel. Her name's Muriel — after her mother. She's personal secretary to Ken Murray, your agent.

Rowan I don't know any ... secretary ... Oh yes ... Blonde girl ... glasses ... on the tall side ...

Willet Brunette. No glasses. Short. You see you do know her! Give me back my wife.

Rowan I've only just gone to Murray — changing agents is about as useful as changing deckchairs on the *Titanic* — but we live in hope. So I couldn't know your Muriel. I don't even wish to know your Muriel.

Willet Oh, something wrong with her? Not good enough for the likes of you? You've got your snout in the trough so you look down your nose at ordinary people. Please, please give me back my wife!

Rowan I think I'll get a nice restful job as a night-nurse in a psychotic ward. Please, Mr Willet, I've got no time!

Willet You've got no time? You've got time for pleasure, time to smash my life to pieces. I'm going to the papers. I'll make a scandal.

Rowan I wish you would. My press agent complains I'm too dull. When I was married he said, "If you won't publicize the wedding, at least divorce her before your next show opens so I can do a piece on that." Believe me, Mr Willet, I don't know your wife.

Willet I didn't believe you when you were acting so why should I believe you when you're not? Nobody knows the trouble I've seen but I'm going to tell them. I've got a slipped disc, migraine, I've lost my wife and if I don't get seven hours sleep a night I'm asthmatic. Oh sir, sir, Napoleon couldn't think of anything during the retreat from Moscow except rushing off to Warsaw to spend a night with his Polish mistress and I can't think of anything else when I'm working at North Acton Borough Council except Muriel. I used to be the bright chap with the ideas in the office. Now I don't rock the boat. I remember the security that goes with the job. Muriel married me for security. We started off in a lovely single room — on a clear day you could see right across it. Now we've got a semi-detached, we go to evening classes twice a week, church on Sunday and have a very active sex life. We were happy and respectable until you came along.

Rowan I'm sure you didn't bother to check before you came staggering in here. Of course you didn't. He's an actor, capable of anything! Words like "theatrical", "melodramatic", "stagey", "putting on an act" are words of abuse. Poker-arsed moralists've been thundering against us for years as role-players, agents of instability, dangerous radicals. It doesn't matter that most actors consider themselves non-political and therefore stand a little to the right of Louis XIV. Everybody's against us because Society likes its citizens to have fixed roles. That way they can be kept in their place. But actors have no place; we keep changing; assume different disguises; imitate other people.

Willet You're doing it now. You're imitating me! I'm the one who's paranoid. You can't go around saying everyone's against you. Everyone's against me, not you, not you. It's always you, you. You've got it easy, soft beds and softer pillows. If you were in a bottle I wouldn't pull out the stopper to give you air. I can't fight champagne for breakfast and lunch at the Garrick. You've got everything, I've got nothing, except Muriel.

Rowan Your grapes're so sour I can smell them from here. Off stage my life isn't silk dressing-gown, competing egos, "dear boys and laddies" and the vowels going "boing, boing" — it's as ordinary as yours. That's why I'm an actor, because when I'm acting I live a different reality from my own — nobler, happier, bolder. Like everybody else I see visions very rarely. I started off as an electrician's mate, got bored and went to drama school. I was lucky they were big on the working class that year. The great thing about drama schools is that however clumsy or misshapen you are there're always others even clumsier and more misshapen queuing behind you. I was going to turn the universe purple every evening. Instead I found myself in front of audiences who resembled delegates from the local mortuary in their winding sheets. But thanks to television, I've ended up with a wife, three kids, two cars, a mother-in-law and a house in Islington to support. I worry about the mortgage, rates, school uniforms, old age and work, which I grab whilst I can. Today the audience is at your feet, tomorrow it could be at your throat. I don't want your wife. I don't want the daily platitudes. I want the lifting vision. I want to act well. I haven't time for my wife, let alone your wife. You've got it wrong. There's nothing wrong.

Willet (*triumphantly handing him a note*) Nothing? Is this note nothing? I found it in Muriel's drawer. I can't read her mind so I read her mail. It's addressed to you.

Rowan (*reading*) "Darling Alec. I will call for you at the theatre tomorrow night. All my deepest love. Muriel."

Willet Give me back my wife ...! (*He groans*) You hear that, you hear that ...? A muttered groan is all that's left of once-proud screaming.

Rowan Interesting.

Willet Interesting? You're a cold cod-fish. I have proof of your adultery with my wife and all you can say is, "interesting".

Rowan How were you and your wife getting on?

Willet What damn business is it of yours? Haven't you done enough? We were getting on marvellously, wonderfully, extraordinarily.

Rowan Marvellously? Wonderfully? Extraordinarily?

Willet Well ... reasonably. I mean we had our problems. Muriel wanted novelties, she thought the sex part was getting too straight up and down ... why the hell am I telling you about Muriel and me?! You probably know already!

Rowan Your relationship was becoming routine. She wanted to do something about it.

Willet And she did!

Rowan Not in the way you think. (*He hands back the note*) Ask yourself, why did she write that? If we were meeting why didn't she just tell me or phone? People phone nowadays, they don't write notes for other people to find. And Muriel doesn't sound the careless type.

Willet She isn't. She always puts the cap back on the toothpaste.

Rowan So how did she come to leave an incriminating note about? Because she wanted you to find it. She wanted to make you jealous. I've had this before.

Willet You have?

Rowan I don't see myself as a star, my nights're too cloudy, but because of my work in television I sometimes become part of the sexual fantasies of people I've never met. Have you found any of my love-letters to your wife?

Willet Ahhhh it's true! You wrote her love-letters. Give me back my wife!

Rowan I haven't written her love-letters but you might find some. That's the next step. She'll write herself a few, sign my name and make sure you find them.

Willet It's ridiculous.

Rowan But it's worked. You've thought more about your wife over the last week than you have for years.

Willet Can't think of anything else; it's blacked out whole days.

Rowan And there's the thrill of intrigue and danger she's created.

Willet And the pain. What about the pain?

Rowan That's part of the excitement too. Pain and jealousy warm desire — open doors.

Willet It's all been a game?

Rowan She wants love so high-powered it causes earthquakes. Remember she's done it because she thinks it'll help your marriage. So try and be understanding when you tell her you know everything.

Willet Tell her? I'm not going to tell her! I'm as good an actor as she is — better. I was at a disadvantage before. Didn't know I was in a play so I was playing for real. Now I know it's a game I can do the part justice. Come to 15A Acadia Street, North Acton any evening, Mr Rowan, and you'll see real acting. All the fighting and the passion, all the suffering and the loving — it'll be magnificent! ... I came here because I thought you'd wrecked a marriage but you've helped save one ... enough said ... I thank you ... Muriel thanks you ... we both thank you ... (*He grabs Rowan's hand, shakes it and moves off, rehearsing to himself*) Muriel, Muriel, Muriel, we can't go on this way ... You must choose ... I'll kill myself if you don't give him up ... Kill myself ...

Willet exits

As the door bangs shut behind him Rowan gives a long drawn out cry of triumph

Rowan Aiiiieeeee! I could sell electric fans to Eskimos! I'm an actor! ... (*He falls on his knees and prays with intense conviction*) Lying lips are an abomination to the Lord. Christ said, "I am the Truth". Yet our lives are raised on lies and a wise man questions every statement except the legitimacy of his own birth. Save us, Lord, I feel an Apocalypse coming on. For a liar usurps God's prerogative and recreates the world in his own image. The moral order's wrecked, objects lose their natural names, force becomes right, right wrong and every treachery an act of friendship ...

BLACK-OUT

FURNITURE AND PROPERTY LIST

On stage: Nil

Personal: **Willet**: note

LIGHTING PLOT

Property fittings required: nil

Interior. The same scene throughout

To open: General lighting

Cue 1   **Rowan**: "... an act of friendship ..."   (Page 42)
            Black-out

EFFECTS PLOT

Cue 1   **Willet** exits   (Page 42)
            Door slam

LAST THINGS

CHARACTERS

Howard Drummond
Lily Drummond

LAST THINGS

A gentle hissing sound in the darkness

A spotlight comes up on a double bed inclined up at the back so we see Howard and Lily Drummond asleep in it

Howard Are you awake?
Lily No.
Howard Are you awake?
Lily I am now.
Howard Don't worry, you haven't got a matinee tomorrow.
Lily What is it?
Howard Listen.
Lily To what?
Howard Just listen.

A long silence

Lily I can't hear anything.
Howard That's it.
Lily That's what?
Howard The silence. Have you ever heard such a silence.

Another long silence

Lily No ... never. No floorboards creaking, no pigeons fluttering on the roof.
Howard No cars starting up in the distance. It's as silent as the grave.

Lily And where's the light? No starlight, moonlight between the
curtains. I can't even see where the window is. No night can be
as black as this.

Howard What's the time ...? Where's the clock ...? Lily ... Lily ...
I can't move ... Can't raise my arms ... Can't turn my head!

Lily Nor me ... Howard, I can't move ... What's happening?

Howard One of us must be dreaming. But I thought I woke up. I
wanted to tell you a nightmare I just had. I dreamed I'd died. I was
lying here like I am now, but dead. And I had this notion
somebody was saying "Ashes to ashes ..." and I was looking up
at mourners at my funeral. I said, "Is this an audience or a
funeral?" and they said, "A funeral!" Everybody was there
including my sister and your brother, Marty, which was a
surprise. The odd thing was I couldn't see you anywhere, Lily. I
know it was only a dream but you could've at least come to my
funeral. They threw dirt into my face, Lily. It was terrible.

Lily Would you like to hear something even worse? I just had
exactly the same dream.

Howard Oh Lord. There's something rotten in the state of Den-
mark.

Lily Don't look at me, I've never been there. I just dreamed I was
laying dead too. And then I saw myself at my own funeral, though
I was still here as well. My brother and your sister, Sarah, were
there. Sarah didn't seem to know whether to laugh or cry ... But
you weren't there. I thought maybe some film producer had
finally called back and you couldn't make it. And there's another
thing — why was your sister there anyway? She'd never come to
my funeral even in a dream.

Howard And your brother would never come to mine.

Lily Can you move?

Howard Not a muscle. It's a short night but we're dreaming a long
dream.

Lily You're sure it is a dream?

Howard What else? I must tell my analyst about it.

Lily Analyst? He's a South American con-man who's more interested in playing the market than being a therapist.

Howard He suits me.

Lily You're too old to have an analyst. You'll never live long enough to finish the treatment. Howard, that's it. I don't think we're both dreaming. I think we're both dead.

Howard Dead? How can we be dead? I know about dead. I've died in some of the best theatres in the world. What makes you say we're dead?

Lily I feel like I'm dead.

Howard Yes ... me too ... But both of us?

Lily It would account for the funeral. And for Marty and Sarah. It's the only social event I could see them both coming to.

Howard I was upset there for a moment — you not turning up. Not like you at all. Dead would explain it.

Lily But both of us at the same time?

Howard How did we manage it?

Lily We didn't do anything out of the ordinary last night, did we? What did we talk about?

Howard The theatre, what else? You said that Gladys Cooper had the most beautiful hands you'd ever seen. And I said, "Yes, but were they her own?"

Lily No, no, wait — what was the last thing we spoke about before we went to sleep?

Howard I asked you if you'd switched the oven off?

Lily I didn't know and you were going to take a look. Did you?

Howard I can't remember. Maybe I did. On the other hand, I was very tired.

Lily That's it then! It's that damn oven. I knew it would get us in the end. We've been gassed.

Howard Gassed?!

Lily And it's your fault.

Howard My fault? You left it on in the first place.

Lily And you should've turned it off. In future when you talk to me start the conversation with "goodbye".

Howard What can I say?

Lily In English not much.

Howard Pardon me for living.

Lily I don't think you are anymore.

Howard At least we were killed. I always disliked the idea of dying.

Lily What happens now?

Howard Tomorrow morning they'll find us lying here stark dead.

Lily Howard, have you got clean underwear on?!

Howard No, I'm in my pyjamas. Lily, can it really be true?

Lily I'm trembling and I can't feel myself trembling ... Are we gone ...? Last bow ...? Final curtain?

Howard And everybody else we know alive and enjoying themselves?

Lily Why us? A critic once wrote we were immortal. But critics never get anything right.

Howard Everything ends. Even the longest run.

Lily But we've so much more to do. After MGM's *Befuddled* we never really made it in the movies like we should have done. It's too late now. What a terrible thing to say —"It's too late now." Howard, I can't breathe! But then if we're dead I couldn't, could I?

Howard No warning, that's the hardest part. No chance to put our lives in order. Nobody told us we were going to die. No inner voice whispered "It's coming, it's coming." And I've always believed in that inner voice. It told us to go into the Duke of York's and not the Shaftesbury. This time it failed. No chance to prepare a few memorable last words. I think my last words were "Goodnight, my dear, switch off the light." Succinct enough, I suppose, and you could read some significance in it if you wanted to. "Put out the light and then put out the light", etc., etc. But if I'd've had the chance I'd've come up with something really good like "Die, my dear doctor, that's the last thing I shall do."

Lily At least we were spared an old people's home.

Howard If we are both dead you realize what a sensation it'll be? The two of us going at the same time. Maybe we were never as big as the biggest. But not even the biggest could beat that exit — "Lily and Howard Drummond Dying As They Lived—Together."

Lily Could make the front pages on a slow day. We've been around a long time, Howard.

Howard Remember our very first meeting? Sidney Worth's *Follies*. Eastbourne Pier. The opening night party.

Lily You came across with a bowl of salted peanuts and said "I wish they were diamonds". We were in competition with Professor Hamilton's "Wonder Show", Chang the Chinese Giant, Miss Elsie Krup the Human Match, who lit gas-rings with her fingers, and Jack O'Riley, the Irish fish-eater who could eat, smoke and drink underwater.

Howard The best of beginnings, my dear. The next year we played Scarborough. We stayed at the old Fisherman's Arms. Burned down later by a drunken chef from Hove who locked himself in the ladies' loo. Ah, those Saturday nights at the Fisherman's with the lobby full of actors running down better ones and the dancers and comics going through their routines. Remember Lilly Tush, Dancer Extraordinaire?

Lily Yes, when I first saw her I thought she must've thrown her jockey.

Howard The fabulous Bobo Brothers and the Announcer saying "We look forward in the near future to doing an entire programme about them."

Lily The night Charlie White and Minty Ryan tried to top each other's jokes and then Tommy Logan rushed in crying and telling them his house had just caught fire, his wife and kids had second-degree burns, he wasn't insured and the police suspected him of arson and Charlie White said "You think that's funny? Just listen to this!"

Howard The things you remember when you're laying in the dark, dead. Bernard Fullerton standing in front of a mirror and saying "Call it vanity, call it narcissism, call it egomania but I love you." No, we're on the edge of eternity, Lily, our eyes waiting to be touched with fingers of fire, our souls poised for the long flight south. It's last things, Lily. We shouldn't be talking shop.

Lily Why not, we always do? We were conceived in a green room, born in a prop casket, educated by a prompter, lived our whole lives on a stage. What else should we talk about?

Howard Things profound, serious, meaningful.

Lily Like what?

Howard Like something out of *Peer Gynt*.

Lily Never could make that play work. Let's face it, my dear, comedy was what we were best at.

Howard I did play *Hamlet*.

Lily Yes, but Maude Jenkins was right, you weren't built for it.

Howard Maude Jenkins was in no position to criticize, jerking about the stage as though she was winnowing corn with her buttocks.

They laugh

Lily Basil Dean once said the public don't want to think, they want to laugh. Look at Ibsen.

Howard "So we looked at Ibsen. He'd just come in and ordered a coffee and Danish with sauerkraut on the side ..." Brilliant routine that. Who says you can't play comedy in the dark — or even dead?

Lily You can play comedy in a sack provided the lines are funny. And the audience can hear you.

Howard Oh yes, the audience has got to hear you. But Lily, this is no time for comedy. If there's a moment to be serious, this is it.

Lily It's hard to change the habits of a lifetime, Howard. We've been terrified of reality and what it leads to.

Howard I'm sure that's why we've been given this last chance to reassess our lives ... add up the pluses and minuses before we meet whoever, whatever. Trouble is, we haven't much experience in dealing with situations like this. Perhaps if we hadn't been so antireligious, it'd be easier.

Lily Anti-religious? Not me. I once played a very superior Mother Superior.

Howard What about that born-again Christian who burst into your dressing-room to tell you he'd been screwed up on drugs and booze but had found God and now he wanted to share Him with you. And you said "Why? You didn't share your drugs and booze." That joke probably blasted our slim chance of salvation.

Lily But we've always thought salvation's well lost for a good joke. You once told a Catholic priest to say three Hail Marys and sixteen cowled coughs and sighs. It's too late to be thinking of kneeling, the show's over. The notices are already out.

Howard "The Real Repertory Company production of 'The Life of Lily and Howard Drummond' was a short and witty comedy, well-suited to the talented company. The theme of two actors unable to distinguish between the stage and life was rich in comic potential but lacking in depth and humanity. Howard Drummond was convincing as the humorous, intelligent husband whilst Lily Drummond was as delightfully sympathetic as ever as his wife. Marty Phipps scored heavily as her no-good brother and mention must be made of Sarah Drummond as the sister. The settings were excellent and the direction adequate after a slow start. Everyone thought the production would run forever but it unexpectedly closed last night due to the sudden permanent indisposition of the two leading players. The theatre is now dark and is liable to remain so."

Lily There's no need to be depressing just because we're dead. I don't feel like apologizing for our lives. Maybe we never had enough of those slow days that build up the past. Oh, but the glitter and the fun of it, what we did and what we saw ... That old hermit in Marrakesh dressed in a pillow-case who claimed the world was coming to an end and, when I objected, sold me a box of figs? And what about that black, half-naked dwarf in the pink fright-wig singing "Danny Boy"?

Howard Yes, we met extraordinary people, but I think we only really lived on stage. Remember when we stayed with Freddy Stiers in his gingerbread house in the South of France and he took us up that mountain for the view? We looked down at the terraces below and the expanse of golden sand and the blue sea and he said, "Isn't it beautiful?"

Lily And you said, "No, it reminds me of rows and rows of empty seats."

Howard That's what I mean. All our roads led back to the theatre — I must be dead, I keep using the past tense! Nothing was ever real, 'til now.

Lily It was real! The laughter was real and the tears. We wept real tears once. When Bobby was knocked down by a bus ... They were real tears.

Howard Yes, they were real.

Lily I never found anyone in the world I could love as much as the audience, except you and Bobby. Sixteen years old ... It seemed such a little bruise and he walked around with it for days, laughing and smiling, and then stopped with a sigh, fell, stretched out, bled and died.

Howard I know, my dear.

Lily In the middle of a performance when we got the news ... Carried on through ... "Twice Two" was one of our biggest hits ... Never missed a laugh.

Howard "I'm sorry, Gertrude, I just had a tooth out."

Lily "Does it hurt?"

Howard "I don't know, the dentist still has it."

Lily "Jeffrey, I've just had an extraordinary experience. I saw this man with one leg standing at a bus stop and I looked at my two legs and then at his one leg and I thought, God you must be rubbish at table-tennis."

Howard Our son was dead and yet the laughs kept coming. Why were we so funny when we were suffering so much? Didn't they see the pain? Were we such good actors? I thought the play would never end that night though Stage Management told us later we'd cut six minutes off the running time. We should've brought down the curtain.

Lily Why? He was dead, like we are now, and nothing would have brought him back. We're here and he was there, laid out cold like us. People were laughing but it didn't change our grief.

Howard We even turn that back into theatre. After Bobby died we started playing Chekhov, didn't we? Soon we didn't know where real sorrow stopped and acting sorrow began, making the real unreal, so it seemed real ...

Lily But my heart broke and if mine did, so did yours.

Howard Did we love each other because we acted so well together, or did we act so well together because we loved each other? Who cares? You were the most exciting person I ever knew. I've never been out of love with you but why did you love me?

Lily You could always make me laugh when I didn't feel like laughing. Give me that toothpaste commercial again.

Howard You mean Agitation toothpaste? ... "Agitation, that amazing blend of molasses, tea-leaves and gum-resin. Private tests by our own house-trained scientists have shown that Agitation contains no single ingredient that would kill a human being and even if it did the acid in your stomach would remove all traces. Agitation is the toothpaste that attacks the gums and says no to BO. It's so healthy and we've got tons of the stuff. Help us get rid of it."

Lily (*laughing*) No wonder I loved you.

Howard I knew it couldn't be my looks. I've always wanted to do something about my face. It looks like you have to feed it peanuts.

Lily Listen to yourself. Doesn't it sound familiar? The same old nerves, the same old doubts and fears. You were always like this opening a new show. You're treating this last night like a first night.

Howard And you're being as calmly infuriating as usual.

Lily Why not? We've nothing to fear. We gave more than we took.

Howard We were never serious, not now, not then ... But you must enjoy life, in spite of life, and if it isn't enjoyable, redo it. We did, didn't we? And if we stand condemned for it, we stand condemned together. If we go down because of it, we'll go down together and Hell will be a Paradise if you're there with me.

Lily And Heaven will be Hell if you're not.

There is a faint whirling sound

Howard Lily, what's that light?

Lily Maybe it's angel light.

Howard It's our last spot, before we're shrouded in oblivion. How do we go out?

Lily Not in silence. Nothing's worse.

Howard With laughter and applause then, even if it is only from angels.

Lily We haven't much time left.

Howard Let's give them our Husband and Wife sketch.

Lily The one we did for the "Night of A Hundred Stars"? That's good ... "Gerald, can you see something different about me?"

Howard "Different, Melissa? Yes, you've put on weight. You've got red blotches and great bags under the eyes. Your neck's gone all scraggy and you've lost what's left of your hair. I don't think I've missed anything. Nothing much gets past me."

Lily "No, you're as sharp as a billiard ball. But you have missed something."

Howard "Oh yes, that Smith and Wesson revolver you're holding — that's new."

Lily "Yes, Gerald, and it's pointing straight at you!"

They burst out laughing despite themselves

Howard Stop corpsing or we'll die out here.

They shriek with laughter as the spot grows brighter

Howard } (*singing*   "Dad nobbles the horses
Lily   }   *together*)   Ma is into blackmail and sin
                                  Auntie Maud is a high-priced hooker,
                                  My God how the money rolls in."

The sound of angels laughing and applauding as the light grows in intensity to a blinding brightness, then suddenly snaps off

Darkness and silence

FURNITURE AND PROPERTY LIST

On stage: Double bed

LIGHTING PLOT

Property fittings required: nil

Interior. The same throughout

To open: Bring up spot on **Howard** and **Lily** in double bed

Cue 1   **Howard** and **Lily**: ' " ... the money rolls in.' "   (Page 56)
            Increase intensity of spot to blinding brightness;
            then black-out

EFFECTS PLOT

Cue 1   To open   (Page 47)
            Gentle hissing in background

Cue 2   **Lily**: " ...if you're not."   (Page 55)
            Faint whirring sound

Cue 3   **Howard** and **Lily**: "" ... the money rolls in.'"   (Page 56)
            Angels laughing and applauding